THE OECD AND THE CHALLENGES OF GLOBALISATION

The governor of the world economy

Written by Ariane de Saeger

Translated by Ciaran Traynor

THE OECD

- **Creation**: the Organisation for Economic Co-operation and Development (OECD) was established in 1961 and grew out of the Organisation for European Economic Co-operation (OEEC), which was created in 1948, just a few years after the Second World War. When it was set up, the OECD's main objective was the application of the Marshall Plan, which aimed to reconstruct Europe and had already been adopted by the United States. Once this was done, a new challenge arose: attempting to improve economic relations between member countries.
- **Main activities**: with 35 member states, the OECD's primary mission is to promote better social and economic policies on a global scale and, consequently, to provide governments with cross-disciplinary analyses and recommendations in order to ensure:
  - restored confidence in the markets by governments, institutions and banks;
  - healthy public finance as the basis of all sustainable economies;
  - universal access to new skills and the acquisition of new sources of growth, in order to ensure the creation of innovative strategies which not only enable the advancement of developing countries, but are also environmentally stable.
- **Key words:**
  - Development: in the strict economic sense of the word, development means the improvement and qualitative and sustainable progress of an economy and

its functioning. However, nowadays "development" often takes on broader meaning, encompassing human development, social development, political development, environmental development, and so on.

- Economic cooperation: a series of mutual aid and trade policies between two or more states in order to promote economic development.
- Free market: a market where buyers and sellers can trade freely according to the price and quantity that they want. Successive financial and economic crises have sometimes got the better of a less free, "more regulated" market. A market economy is an economy where all trade is unregulated, the state does not interfere and the demand and the offers of economic agents are all that matter.
- Free trade: the opposite of protectionism, free trade is a concept which calls for the suppression of all tariff barriers (customs duties) and obstacles to international exchange and transactions.
- Globalisation: from an economic point of view, globalisation reflects the evolution of the worldwide integration of economic, ecological, financial and cultural phenomena in a unified economic and commercial system. In other words, while in the past economies developed alone (on a national, regional or local scale), today they are linked and evolve together in a "globalised" economy.
- Governance: a way of governing and administrating. In this particular context, we are talking specifically about democratic governance. This notion goes beyond the traditional framework of public action and

focuses on new forms of civic responsibility. The state remains the main actor, but it is no longer alone.

- The International Monetary Fund (IMF): founded in 1944, the IMF is an organisation charged with ensuring financial stability on an international scale. It is also a specialised institution of the UN. In concrete terms, this means that it monitors the correct implementation of exchange rates and lends foreign currency to countries which cannot pay for their imports. Over time, it has become the "last-hope lender" for the poorest, most indebted countries.

- Liberalisation or privatisation: an action which makes trade freer by reducing the intervention of the state. It is therefore possible to liberalise a whole sector or economy. For example, the liberalisation of the water sector would mean that it was no longer managed by the state (or public institutions) but by private companies.

- Sustainable development: a model of development through which the needs of both the current generation and future generations are entirely satisfied. The three interdependent components of sustainable development are the environmental, social and economic dimensions.

- The United Nations (UN): an international organisation founded in 1945 that includes almost every country in the world. It works towards world peace and aims to aid and strengthen cooperation with regard to international law, international security, social progress, economic development and human rights.

- The World Bank: founded in 1944, the World Bank now

includes five institutions (IBRD, IDA, IFC, MIGA and ICSID) and is an organ of the United Nations. It is made up of 189 member states. Its role is to financially assist developing countries in sectors such as education, health, agriculture and industry.

At times fiercely criticised and at others showered with praise, globalisation is a hot topic. It is much debated: according to some, it imposes a mishmash of economies while eliminating the weakest countries or removing all commercial barriers in order to liberalise trade for the benefit of the few. In any case, it is undeniable that it plays a part in economic trade and can sometimes spectacularly increase profit. However, in the end, are globalisation and organisations which favour free trade and an integrated global economy really in the best interests of everyone?

Given the extremely critical, even worrying situation in many countries, it is essential to reconsider what has already been established by previous generations. In order to do so, we can take a look back into our collective past to better understand the evolution of this commercial and economic context, which began to liberalise after the end of the Second World War and which continues to this day.

> Why was the establishment of an organisation like the OECD judged to be pertinent at the time? What role does it play within our worldwide, globalised economy? Would it be possible to do without it nowadays? How would trade change?

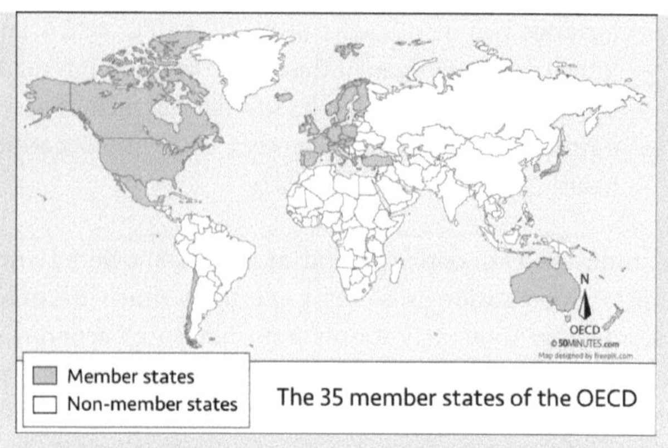

Australia, Austria, Belgium, Canada, Chile, the Czech Republic, Denmark, Estonia, Finland, France, Germany, Greece, Hungary, Iceland, Ireland, Israel, Italy, Japan, Latvia, Luxembourg, Mexico, Norway, New Zealand, the Netherlands, Poland, Portugal, Slovakia, Slovenia, South Korea, Spain, Sweden, Switzerland, Turkey, the United Kingdom and the United States.

CONTEXT

ECONOMIC RECOVERY AFTER THE SECOND WORLD WAR

The Marshall Plan, the OEEC and the OECD

After the Second World War, Europe was determined not to repeat the errors of the past and wanted to encourage lasting peace based on cooperation and reconstruction. The OEEC was therefore set up in 1948 to ensure the correct application of the Marshall Plan.

<u>**WHAT WAS THE MARSHALL PLAN?**</u>

The Marshall Plan was an economic recovery plan proposed by the American Secretary of State George C. Marshall (1880-1959). It was financed by the United States and came into effect in 1948, under the presidency of Harry S. Truman (1884-1972). The plan, which was entrusted to the OEEC to carry out, was initially supposed to last four years and help Europe to regain a degree of economic and financial stability.

The success of the organisation interested the United States and Canada, and so they signed a charter on 14 December 1960, which resulted in the creation of the Organisation for Economic Co-operation and Development (OECD) on 30 September of the following year. Other countries, including Japan, Brazil and India, then joined the institution and in the space of 50 years, its initiatives and advances were bearing promising fruits. For example, the United States tripled its national wealth. Other countries that for a long time had played nothing more than a minor role on the international stage now became important players in a future sustainable economy – particularly China, India, Brazil, South Africa and Indonesia.

Free trade and the establishment of post-war international organisations

THE NEW INTERNATIONAL DIVISION OF LABOUR: THE BASIS OF FREE TRADE

Why should international trade be liberalised? Let us take the hypothesis that a country's wealth is the result of the division of labour between its inhabitants.

The division of labour corresponds to the distribution and specialisation of the production process. For example, if an individual is a specialist in farming, it will be in the best interests of the community (the region or the country) to have specialists in other domains. Even if this observation is somewhat simplistic, it cannot be denied that the division of labour creates wealth.

This principle can be applied on a community, national or even international level: it is in the best interests of a country to produce goods or services to meet a particular demand and at the same time take advantage of other countries' produce for other goods. This is called the new international division of labour, which can be limited to a certain extent if countries create obstacles (such as tariff barriers). Although the world is commercially and economically liberalising, businesses and governments in many countries have practices which go against free trade.

The Wall Street Crash of 1929 and the Second World War obviously made the world's countries rethink the way they interact with one another. It was now clear that there was a desperate need for more international trade. In 1944, the Bretton Woods Conference brought together the representatives of 44 nations to work out an international economic recovery plan with three fundamental pillars:

- economic investment,
- financial management,
- the organisation of trade.

The first two pillars were realised through the creation of the World Bank and the International Monetary Fund. A new organisation called the World Trade Organisation (WTO) was supposed to see to the third pillar, which aimed to boost the economy through a new wave of trade and commerce.

A number of negotiations, partly due to the tension caused by the Second World War and the Cold War, with the great powers of the business world unfortunately led to such diverging points of view that the WTO was not founded at that time. Instead, a provisional agreement called the GATT was signed and remained in place for around 47 years, until the long-awaited creation of the WTO in 1994.

THE GATT

The General Agreement on Tariffs and Trade was an international agreement signed in 1947 which included a collection of treaties, rules and directives to establish a common framework for the creation of "free trade" between the different countries of the world. Its objective was to reduce customs duties, renegotiate – or even eliminate – all tariff and other barriers and encourage international trade. Its fundamental principles were:

- stable customs duties;
- the general elimination of quantitative restrictions on international trade;
- the introduction the principle of the most favoured nation (in other words, an advantage given to a member becomes an advantage for all members);
- national treatment (which involves treating all nations the same);
- the generalised system of preferences (a system in which industrialised countries offer non-reciprocal preferential treatment to less industrialised countries);
- the law of retaliation, illustrated perfectly by the expression "an eye for an eye", and sanctions.

The appearance of the WTO

The World Trade Organisation (WTO) was set up in 1995, after the Marrakesh Agreement in 1994, to make up for the failings of the GATT. Made up of 164 countries and representing more than 95% of international trade, it is the only international organisation which governs trade regulations between countries.

Although the WTO is run by member governments, which also ratify its laws and treaties, the organisation would fall apart without the dedicated work of its Secretariat, which coordinates all its activities, encourages dialogue between members and ensures the application and respect of trade regulations.

The tasks of the WTO are many and varied:

- trade negotiations,
- establishment and monitoring of trade policies adopted by the members of the WTO,
- the settling of arguments and differences,
- communication,
- increasing the trade capabilities of governments who wish it.

Moreover, the WTO and the OECD actively cooperate with one another. While the WTO is perceived as a reference institution which governs international trade to ensure greater coherence and harmony on the world stage, the OECD focuses more on commercial aid and, more particularly, on the strengthening of trade capacity.

THE FIRST SIGNS OF GLOBALISATION

Although the period following the Second World War saw great change in economic and commercial exchange, this was partly to the detriment of the economic development of the poorest countries. However, certain countries were the exception to the rule and managed to make the best of a bad situation.

- Economies such as those of South Korea and Taiwan managed to export their goods to industrialised countries, thanks to technology and capital from the United States and Japan.
- We observe the same tendency among oil-rich countries, which reinvested their profits in production sectors in developed countries.

However, these few successes of countries in the South in the process of globalisation are far from an overall reflection of the complexity of the situation.

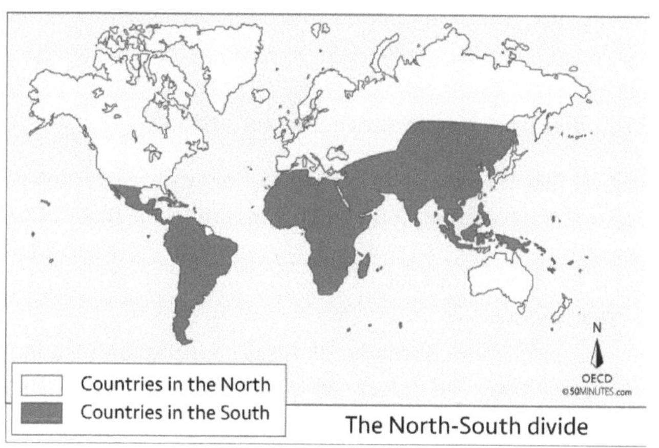

The North-South divide

WHERE DOES THE TERM "DEVELOPING COUNTRIES" COME FROM?

The difference between countries in the "North" and the "South" began to increase at the start of the 1970s, and the terms associated with them evolved over time as a result: nowadays, they are generally known as "developing countries" although, since the Cold War, they have also sometimes been called "Third World countries". However, since the term "developing countries" has come under fire for being too negative, it began to be replaced by the notion of "periphery countries" at the end of the 20th century. This term is based on trade and is considered less controversial. Finally, countries in the South tend to belong to the "developing" category, while those in the North are judged to already be "developed".

Globalisation, dependence and evolution

Several factors have gone in favour of or against the globalisation of developing countries compared to the rest of the world.

- **The brakes**
  - Colonisation: formerly colonised countries only traded with their old rulers, which led to them becoming relatively commercially dependent. Once they are deprived of their guardians, many colonised countries do not manage to become completely independent, because over time their dependence has become essential to their own economic development.
  - The supremacy of great powers: industrialised countries have always traded amongst themselves, with developing countries left on the sidelines and often forced to depend on their relationship with developed countries.
- **The accelerator**
  - Spectacular growth: although developing countries accounted for a quarter of global trade at the beginning of the 20th century, they became a much bigger presence in the second half of the 20th century, making up almost 40% of all trade thanks to the spectacular growth of certain regions (particularly in Latin America and in Asia, where countries went through heavy industrialisation, significant demographic transition or a notable improvement in living conditions).

The Prebisch–Singer hypothesis, or, the regrettable consequences of dependency theory

According to the theory of international trade as developed by the British economists Adam Smith (1723-1790) and David Ricardo (1772-1823) claims that:

- a country's revenue can increase through trade;
- it is in every country's interest to specialise in the exportation of products in which it has an advantage in terms of production costs (the theory of comparative advantage);
- free trade implies an international division of labour which is beneficial to all (access to a larger market and greater production of goods thanks to more factors of production);
- over time, technological development brings about a decrease in the price of industrial products for the benefit of the producers of raw material.

In 1950, Raúl Prebisch (Argentinian economist, 1901-1986) denounced the devastating effects of the free market. In his view, the terms of trade between rich and poor countries are only ever in favour of developed countries, thereby making life difficult for the poorest states. There are many explanations for this, but here are a few main ones:

- The prices of manufactured, industrial products remain high, mainly because of the monopolies which can sustain them on one hand, and the unions which allow pay increases thanks to the increase of product prices on the other hand.
- The terms of trade of raw materials deteriorate, which means that developing countries import less (manufactured products, since they increase in value) and export more (raw materials, whose value falls).

Oil crises and price drops in raw materials over the course of history confirm Prebisch's findings. His theory is also strengthened by factual arguments which justify the imbalance or even the deterioration of trade due to liberalisation.

The imbalance of international trade

Arguments which show upward pressure on the prices of products in the North, thereby preventing trade between the countries in the South and the most powerful countries and regions of the globe	Arguments which prove that the price in products in the South decreases
• <u>Unionisation and work:</u> in the 1970s, the high level of unionisation of workers combined with full employment meant that people in rich countries saw their salaries increase. This widespread payrise then led to an increase in productivity as well as the price of products. • <u>Innovation and sophistication:</u> Industrialised, technologically advanced counties began to develop sophisticated, and therefore more expensive, products. • <u>The offer of competitively priced goods</u> and, consequently, certain luxury items.	• <u>Low-quality products:</u> goods exported by countries in the South are often the result of a basic, rather crude production process. Their relatively high productivity is not enough to contend with the big players in the raw material market. • <u>The demand for basic materials steadily decreases.</u> Increased incomes in countries in the North give their inhabitants a better quality of life and therefore allow them to deal more in synthetic products rather than in the raw materials sold by the South. • <u>The monopoly of big multinational companies</u> often ruins small producers, who cannot afford to cut prices because of their production costs.

In the decades which followed, every new development on the international scale either disproved or, on the contrary, confirmed the Prebisch–Singer hypothesis, with the price of raw materials rising and falling over time. On the one hand, the creation of OPEC (Organisation of the Petroleum Exporting Countries), for example, does not corroborate this theory with less variable fluctuations thanks to price control. On the other hand, the oil crises at the end of the 20th century confirm this hypothesis. In 1973, after a serious international crisis in the Middle East, oil prices rose from $3 to $10 a barrel. This jump in price was only possible thanks to the high demand from industrialised countries. In this case, the monopoly on oil by several countries (OPEC) confirms Prebisch's hypothesis that the free market deteriorates trade and leaves the weakest worse off.

DID YOU KNOW?

The Organisation of the Petroleum Exporting Countries (OPEC) is an international organisation founded in 1960 whose main goals are the coordination, unification and harmonisation of petroleum policies to protect the interests of its members. For example, it coordinates production in order to maintain price stability in the oil market and avoid drops in price.

Created on the initiative of Venezuela, the OPEC is made up of 14 members: the five founding countries (Iran, Iraq, Kuwait, Saudi Arabia and Venezuela) as well as, in order of entry, Qatar, Libya, the United Arab Emirates, Algeria, Nigeria, Angola, Ecuador, Gabon and Equatorial Guinea.

THE ROLE AND MISSION OF THE OECD

MISSION

The primary mission of the OECD is to improve socio-economic wellbeing throughout the world with its suggestions for adapted policies to implement. In more concrete terms, it:

- offers governments a space where they can discuss and share their respective experience and expertise, in order to find solutions to their common problems;
- works with governments to determine the vectors of economic, social and environmental development, which are the three pillars of sustainable development for all;
- measures productivity and international trade regarding business and investment;
- analyses and compares data and statistics in order to better anticipate future trends and (re)act as appropriate;
- establishes standards in a number of domains (security, chemical products, taxation, etc.);
- analyses the indicators which can have direct repercussions on individuals' well-being (taxes, the cost of living, etc.).

The OECD does not take on this mission alone: it works in partnership with many different organisations concerned with global development and the wellbeing of all. This collaboration involves governments, businesses (the Business and Industry Advisory Committee to the OECD), unions (the Trade Union Advisory Committee) and civil society (the OECD Forum).

THE STRUCTURE OF THE OECD

The Council, the Committees and the Secretariat work across the institution to ensure its smooth running and relay its recommendations to the four corners of the world.

The structure of the OECD

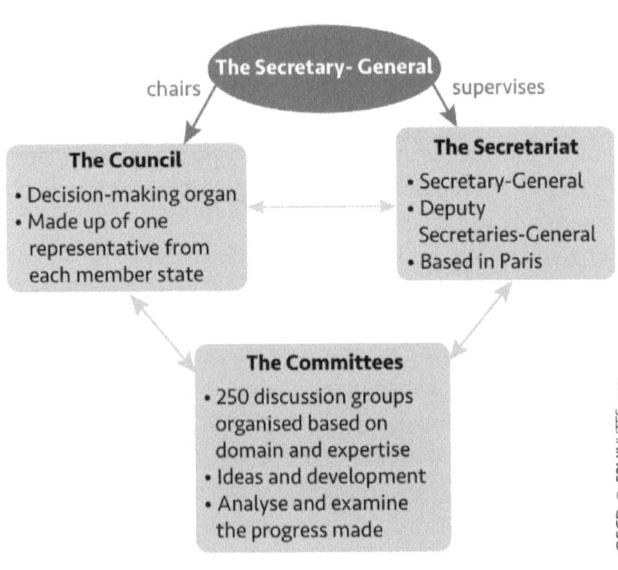

- **The Council** is the decision-marking organ of the OECD and is responsible for the supervision and direction of its overall strategy. All member states (including a representative from the European Commission) are represented with one person per nation: the delegates meet regularly and make decisions together under the leadership of the Secretary-General, who chairs the meeting.
- **The 250 committees** of the OECD correspond to "working groups" made up of senior officials from the 35 member states: they debate potential ideas and progress made in specific domains.
- **The Secretariat**, based in Paris, is led by the Secretary-General (who is elected every five years), who analyses the different proposals made by the committees together with a group of Deputy Secretaries-Generals.

JOSÉ ÁNGEL GURRÍA, THE 5ᵀᴴ SECRETARY-GENERAL OF THE OECD

José Ángel Gurría (Mexican economist and politician, born in 1950) was thrust into the international limelight when he became Secretary-General of the OECD in 2006, having already been the Mexican Secretary of Foreign Affairs (1994-1998) and Secretary of Finance and Public Credit (1998-2000). Highly regarded for putting in place economic mechanisms which saved the Mexican economy (the sector enjoyed a 6.7 % growth rate during his time as Secretary of Finance and Public Credit), Gurría demonstrated his negotiation skills on several occasions and promoted dialogue between America and the rest of the world regarding international issues.

As a minister, he had already established close ties with the OECD, beginning with the joining of Mexico right up to his presidency of the Council in 1999. He succeeded Donald J. Johnston (lawyer and federal deputy from Quebec, born in 1936) and became the 5th Secretary-General of the OECD. In May 2015, his mandate was renewed for the third consecutive time: his career has been characterised by excellence, dynamism and leadership.

FINANCIAL MEANS

In 2016, the OECD's budget increased to 370 million euros. The organisation is entirely financed by its member states, whose national contribution depends on the size of their economy. The United States alone brings in around 21% of the overall figure, making it the biggest donator, well ahead of the remaining countries. Japan is in second place with 10.79%, Germany in third place with 7.52% and the United Kingdom fifth with 5.34%. At the same time, member states can support the results of the programmes put in place by the OECD. Unlike the World Bank or the IMF, the OECD does not give loans or funding

THE OECD'S ACTIONS

The OECD analyses data and transforms it into policies.

The actions of the OECD

Promotion of better social and economic policies
Making available general analyses and recommendations to help governments in order to encourage:

- restored confidence in the markets by governments, institutions and banks

- healthy public finance as the basis of all sustainable economies

- universal access for all to new skills and the acquisition of new sources of growth, in order to encourage the creation of innovative strategies which not only enable the advancement of developing countries, but are also environmentally stable

The OECD's action plan

1. Gather a maximum of factual data in order to evaluate the overall economic situation and thereby identify the progress that has been made.
2. Analyse the data in order to pinpoint future challenges and make short- and medium-term predictions.
3. Discuss all possible scenarios with the OECD members,

and even begin negotiations if necessary; every organ of the OECD participates in its own way in the elaboration of the recommendations to relay to governments.

4. The Council of the OECD makes a decision in order to begin implementing the best solution out of those discussed.
5. Make governments (individually or as one) carry out this solution through a plan of action – standards, policies or agreements which favour economic growth, financial stability and the reduction of poverty.
6. Peer review through a multilateral monitoring system (by governments or special committees) to increase control and transparency. The anti-corruption team, for example, is charged with fighting against the corruption of foreign public agents through international trade.

Working side by side with the G20

The 2008 financial crisis is evidence of the concrete role of the OECD. This turbulent period, which led to many reputable banks going out of business, caused certain countries to go through debt crises and eventually brought about the general collapse of the economy. Although it is perfectly logical to question the pertinence of maintaining the current globalised economic system, how should we interpret the intervention of international organisations which are trying to preserve a certain economic balance?

With the 2008 crisis, it became evident that specialised organisations in the world must act together to face the challenges of modern society. Following this logic, the

G20 called on the data collection and analysis skills of the OECD (as well as other specialised institutions) to facilitate the search for a general, well-thought-out reaction to the financial crisis.

THE CONSTRUCTION OF THE G20

The Group of Twenty (G20) was created in 1999 in response to the financial crises which emerging markets (Brazil, China, India and Russia, also known as the BRIC countries) were suffering from in the 1990s: it came about as a result of the necessity to create an international dialogue involving different representatives of governments and heads of state from all over the world (including developed economies, developing economies and emerging markets). This would be a place to debate recurrent global issues such as rising prices, pensions, employment, and so on.

While its original aim was to encourage international cooperation on economic subjects, it has taken on the role of economic guide since 2008. It makes frequent use of the World Bank, the IMF, the OECD and the WTO in its work and analyses.

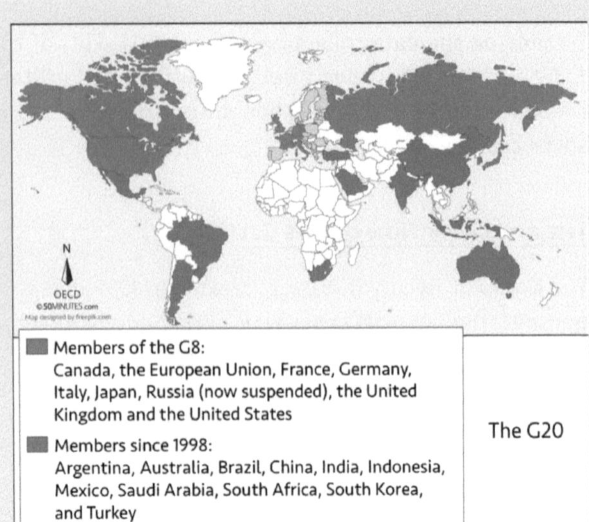

Since this fruitful collaboration, the OECD has actively and regularly intervened on questions dealt with by the G20: it gathers data, submits analyses, makes recommendations, and so on. Its 50 years of experience make it a breeding ground for innovation and policies which address international crises and uncertainties.

With the G20, the OECD works notably on the problem of employment, in partnership with the International Labour Organisation (ILO). These two organisations have carried out specific analyses on this subject, drafted reports and given recommendations. Their principal concerns are universal accessibility, stimulation of small and medium-sized businesses and education and training as gateways to employment.

Together, the OECD and the G20 also act in other domains in order to stimulate the economy and give it a new lease of life (cracking down on tax havens, increasing food and energy products, introducing policies to financially protect consumers, and so on).

IMPACT OF THE OECD

THE OECD IN THE WORLD

Thanks to the organisation's concrete actions and the work of its Secretary-General, the influence of the OECD has completely transformed over the past decade.

The changes the organisation has gone through can be summed up in seven points. The OECD now:

- Helps member states to progress with their reform programmes.
- Builds a fairer, stronger and healthier global economy.
- Is the leading organisation when it comes to deciding which economic policies to introduce.
- Is the hub of international financial standards: corruption, the social responsibility of businesses, taxation, and so on. For example, the G20 and the OECD together managed to put an end to bank secrecy.
- Ensures transparency in all its dealings.
- Targets new geographical areas to acquire new members and forge ties with other international organisations.
- Is a shining example of global leadership.

BELGIUM

There are a number of contrasting opinions when it comes to summing up the OECD's actions and their concrete effects throughout the world. The social and economic context of Belgium and its relationship with the rest of the world is an effective example of the organisation's work on a microeconomic and macroeconomic level.

A study by Petercam (a Belgian financial group) classifies the 35 member states of the OECD according to five criteria: transparency and democratic values, share of wealth and healthcare, education, the environment and the economy. Although Belgium is not doing too badly at all – it was 13th in 2013 – there is still work to be done, mainly in providing jobs to migrants and young people, reducing CO_2 emissions and increasing renewable energy, and reducing debt in the private sector (which is relatively high compared to its neighbours).

According to the OECD, Belgium "is on the right track, but..."

Based on the 2015 OECD report on the economic situation in Belgium, the progress the country has made is still unsatisfactory on the whole: while the deficit has been reduced and measures to improve general wellbeing have been introduced, external growth and competitiveness continues to increase. The OECD highlights that long-term growth is slowed by the low employment rate and erosion of cost competitiveness, while public debt remains high. Moreover, the socio-professional integration of immigrants (regarding jobs and housing conditions) is still a problem. The data gathered on Belgium's economic climate, the resulting analyses and the discussions and negotiations led to three recommendations:

• assure budget viability while encouraging employment

and competition;
- improve the integration of immigrants in the job market;
- maintain the efficacy and fairness of the housing market.

The OECD submitted reform suggestions for each of these three recommendations.

Belgium compared to its neighbours

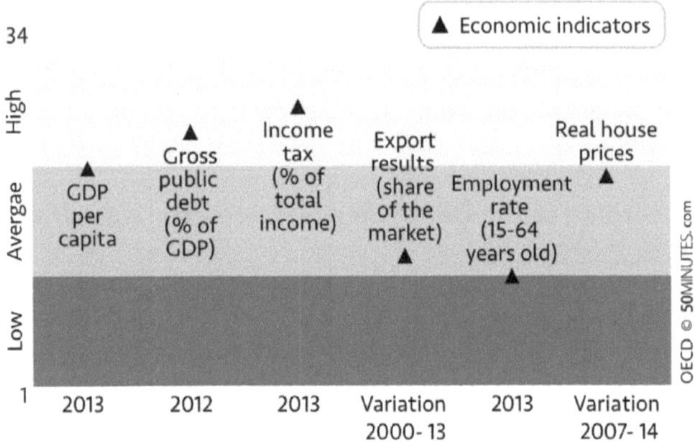

Worrying income inequalities

The OECD also reveals that the difference in income between the rich and the poor is the highest it has been for 30 years. Even though Belgium was behind Denmark in 2013 with a Gini coefficient of 0.27 compared to 0.28 in 2007, statistics show that the top 10% have more 9.6 times more wealth (income) than the bottom 10% of society.

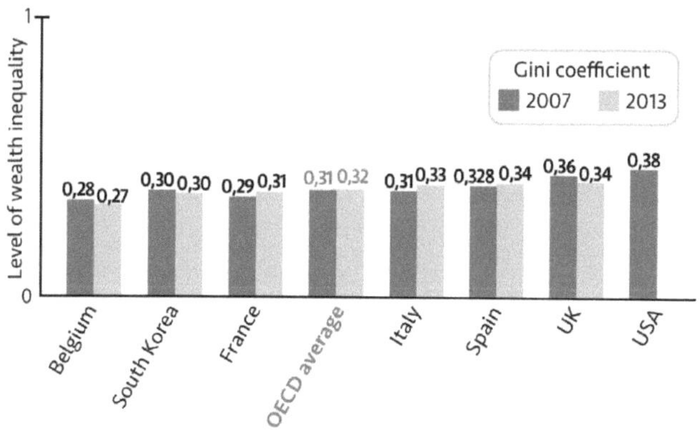

WHAT IS THE GINI COEFFICIENT?

The Gini coefficient is an indicator which measures the level of wealth inequality (income, standard of living, etc.). It varies between 0 and 1: 0 means that a country is totally equal and 1 means that it is completely unequal. Between 0 and 1, the inequality is greater the high the number.

Although these inequalities affect overall social cohesion, they may also impact on long-term economic growth, which is why the OECD advises redistributing collective wealth (through taxes) in the form of benefits.

EMPLOYMENT AND SKILLS: A CHALLENGE FOR THE FUTURE

The OECD calls for equality between men and women and equal opportunities in employment, and urges governments to invest in education and training (free education, for example). This aspect is an important factor of economic and social development.

There are currently around 40 million young people, aged between 15 and 29, in the 35 OECD countries who are not in education, employment or training. Based on a 2015 OECD report entitled *Youth, Skills and Employability*, young people between the ages of 16 and 29 years are twice as likely to find themselves unemployed than adults in the next age bracket. Governments are being called to act to fix this problem and help young people to find a job.

The OECD has also reported major social challenges which must be solved quickly. Wealth inequality between the richest and the poorest, just like the unsatisfactory integration of immigrants on the job market, are not just social problems, but societal issues. If these problems are not solved and reduced now, they will have a negative impact on the growth and the general development of the country.

Across the countries in the OECD, it would appear that:

- 10% of new graduates have little knowledge of literature.
- 14% struggle in mathematical subjects.
- 40% of pupils who drop out in high school have unsatisfactory knowledge of both mathematics and literature.

- Less than 50% of pupils in professional schooling and less than 40% of those in general schooling have the chance to do a work placement. This lack of understanding of the professional world, combined with little practical experience, is too big a risk for companies which are recruiting.

Institutional obstacles (taxes, contributions) also have an impact on youth unemployment, meaning they often find themselves with little job security as they are forced to do part-time or temporary jobs.

SUMMARY

The OECD:

- was created in 1961 as a way to encourage international trade and contribute to the economic development and reconstruction of Europe after the Second World War;
- is made up of 35 member states and 3 organs – the Council, the Secretariat and the Committees – which ensure the smooth running of the institution and relay its recommendations and other analyses to help to effectively put in place new policies;
- set up its Secretariat in Paris and employs 2500 officials;
- finances itself with member subscriptions, the amount of which varies depending on the size of the country;
- aims to help governments implement policies which will lead to economic development and increased wellbeing for all;
- collaborates with member governments, trade unions, universities, associations and international institutions (for example, the G20);
- evaluates each country individually, but also compares them to others;
- considers that Belgium is on the right path but that there is still more to be done as regards employment and competition, the social and professional integration of immigrants and the fairness of the job market;
- will have to face two major problems in the coming years: employment and the skill development of young people and women.

We want to hear from you!
Leave a comment on your online library
and share your favourite books on social media!

FURTHER READING

- Link to the OECD's homepage. http://www.oecd.org/
- Link to the OPEC's homepage. http://www.opec.org/
  opec_web/en/index.htm

BIBLIOGRAPHY

- Brunel, S. (2007) Qu'est-ce que la mondialisation ?
  Sciences Humaines. [Online]. [Accessed 21 June 2017].
  Available from: <https://www.scienceshumaines.com/
  qu-est-ce-que-la-mondialisation_fr_15307.html>
- Clerq, D. (2005) La mondialisation n'est pas coupable.
  Vertus et limites du libre-échange Paul R. Krugman.
  Alternatives économiques. [Online]. [Accessed 25 July
  2015]. Available from: <https://www.alternatives-eco-
  nomiques.fr/la-mondialisation-n-est-pas-coupable-
  -vertus-et-limites-du-libre-echange-paul-r--krug-
  man_fr_art_222_25323.html>
- Degans, A. (2011) Ces pays émergents qui font basculer
  le monde. *Sciences Humaines*. [Online]. [Accessed 21 June
  2017]. Available from: <https://www.scienceshumaines.
  com/ces-pays-emergents-qui-font-basculer-le-
  monde_fr_27711.html>
- De Grandi, M. (2015) Pour l'OCDE, les inégalités de
  revenus dans le monde sont à « un point critique ». *Les
  Échos*. [Online]. [Accessed 21 June 2017]. Available from:
  <https://www.lesechos.fr/22/05/2015/LesEchos/21943-
  029-ECH_pour-l-ocde--les-inegalites-de-revenus-dans-
  le-monde-sont-a---un-point-critique--.htm>

- France Diplomatie. (2012) *Qu'est-ce que le G20 ?* [Online]. [Accessed 21 June 2017]. Available from: < http://www. diplomatie.gouv.fr/fr/politique-etrangere-de-la-france/ diplomatie-economique-et-commerce-exterieur/ peser-sur-le-cadre-de-regulation-europeen-et-interna- tional-dans-le-sens-de-nos/faire-de-la-regulation-inter- nationale-un-atout-pour-l-economie-francaise/article/ qu-est-ce-que-le-g20>
- Grega, P. (2012-2013) Problèmes de gestion dans un contexte de développement. *Développement et Gestion Nord-Sud.* Brussels: ICHEC Brussels Management School.
- Mignon, T. (2015) Rapport de l'OCDE : la Belgique reçoit un bon bulletin, mais... *rtbf.be.* [Online]. [Accessed 21 June 2017]. Available from: <https://www.rtbf.be/ info/economie/detail_rapport-de-l-ocde-la-belgique- recoit-un-bon-bulletin-mais?id=8898558>
- OECD. (2015) Études économiques de l'OCDE. Belgique. *Éditions OCDE.* [Online]. [Accessed 21 June 2017]. Available from: <http://www.keepeek.com/ Digital-Asset-Management/oecd/economics/etudes- economiques-de-l-ocde-belgique-2015_eco_surveys-bel- 2015-fr#page12>
- OECD. (2015) Les gouvernements doivent redoubler d'efforts pour traiter le problème du chômage chez les jeunes. *Éditions OCDE.* [Online]. [Accessed 21 June 2017]. Available from: <http://www.keepeek. com/Digital-Asset-Management/oecd/education/ oecd-skills-outlook-2015_9789264234178-en#page9>
- OECD. (2015) Rapport du secrétaire général aux ministres 2015. *Éditions OCDE.* [Online]. [Accessed 21 June 2017]. Available from: <http://issuu.com/oecd.

publishing/docs/012015102e/13?e=3055080/13238727>

- OECD stat. (2014) *Distribution des revenus et pauvreté.* [Online]. [Accessed 21 June 2017]. Available from: <http://stats.oecd.org/Index.aspx?DataSetCode=IDD&Lang=fr>
- Petercam. (2014) *Communiqué de presse. Classement de durabilité – OECD.* [Online]. [Accessed 21 June 2017]. Available from: <https://www.petercam.com/sites/default/files/news/files/2014_10_17_pr_sri_fr.pdf>
- Universalis. (No date) O.C.D.E. (Organisation de coopération et de développement économiques). *Encyclopædia Universalis.* [Online]. [Accessed 21 June 2017]. Available from: <http://www.universalis.fr/encyclopedie/organisationde-cooperation-et-de-developpement-economiques/>
- Université du Québec à Montréal. (2007) Théorie du développement et du sous-développement. *UQAM.* [Online]. [Accessed 25 July 2015]. Available from: <http://politique.uqam.ca/upload/files/automne2007/notes_des_cours/Pol-4131-20_Cours25SEPT07.pdf>

ADDITIONAL SOURCES

- Krugman, P. (1997) *Pop Internationalism.* Cambridge, Massachusetts: MIT Press.
- Stiglitz, J. (2003) *Globalization and Its Discontents.* London: Penguin.

IMPROVE YOUR GENERAL KNOWLEDGE

IN A BLINK OF AN EYE !

www.50minutes.com